MW00334610

SoundBlendS

Fun Under the Sun

SoundBlends

SoundBlends

Volume Two

Fun Under the Sun

Erin Johnson

A SoundBlendsBook

Copyright 2013
Acadia Press
www.acadiapress.com

All rights reserved. No part of this publication may be reproduced, stored in a retrieval system, or transmitted, in any form or by any means, electronic, mechanical, photocopying, recording or otherwise, without prior written permission from the publisher. No part of this book may be used or reproduced in any manner whatsoever without written permission.

SoundBlendS Volume Two: Fun Under the Sun

ISBN# 978-0-9910458-1-5

www.soundblends.com

Printed in the United States of America

October 2013

Stories

SoundBlendS makes reading easy.

Here is what you need to know.

What You Need to Know

Reading starts with Sounds...

s s s

Some of the English Sounds

a

ee

oo

Vowel Sounds

Consonant Sounds

z

sh

Learn more about the 43 Sounds at www.soundblends.com

What You Need to Know

Sounds and Letter Names are different

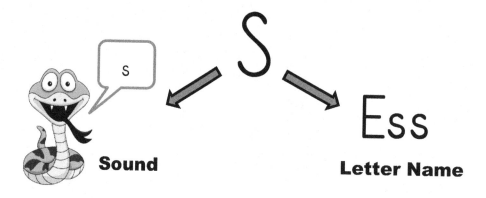

Sound

Letter Name

Letter Names help with Spelling NOT Reading

COW

Say: c + ow

Spell: See Oa Dubul-Yoo

The 26 Letter Names are shown in the More Information on **SoundBlends** *section and on* **www.soundblends.com**

Blend Sounds to say Words...

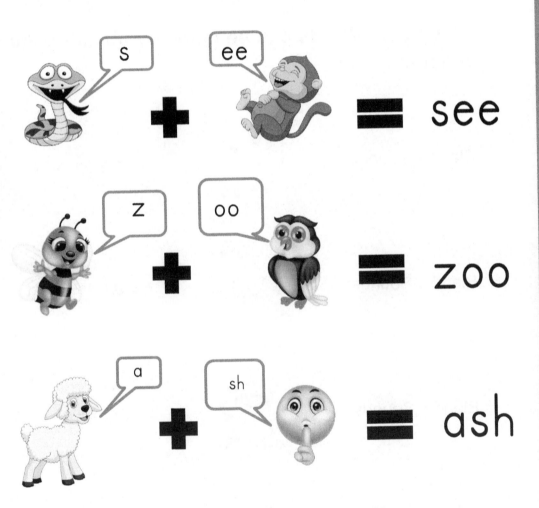

All 43 Vowel and Consonant Sounds as well as the spellings of these Sounds are shown in the More Information on SoundBlendS... section at the back of the book and on the website www.soundblends.com

What You Need to Know

Blend Sounds to say Words...

All English Words can be made by blending the 43 Sounds

Blend 2 Sounds:  c + ow → cow

Blend 3 Sounds:  c + a + t → cat

Blend 4 Sounds: f + r + o + g → frog

Blending Consonant Sounds can be tricky!

What You Need to Know

The Reading Process:

Letters → Sounds → Words...

Simple Reading Process

1. See the Letters

2. Say the Sound

3. Blend the Sounds to say the Word

Learn more at www.soundblends.com

What You Need to Know

SoundBlendS makes reading easy...

Starting simple builds skills and confidence

- ➢ Story #1 uses only 8 simple Sounds
- ➢ Stories #1-5 use only 2 and 3 Sound Words
- ➢ The *most common* Sound for the Letters is taught first
- ➢ The Reading Process is the same for each and every Word throughout the stories

Story sequence progresses systematically

- ➢ Each story introduces new Sounds
- ➢ Stories and sentences become longer with more complex vocabulary
- ➢ Text font size gradually decreases

SoundBlendS builds confident readers!

What You Need to Know

SoundBlendS makes reading easy by...

Using font changes as visual cues

Black Font for Single Letter Sounds

Big dog dug.

Light Gray Font for Letter Groups = 1 Sound

Josh had fresh milk in a glass.

| Letter Group | Letter Group | Sight Word | Letter Group |

Dark Gray Font for the few Sight Words

Visual cues make it easy to read each and every word in these stories.

How to Go Through this Book

See the Letters

Say the Sounds

Blend the Sounds to

say Words

Say the Sounds

Start each Story by Saying the Sounds...

Point at each Letter

Say the Sound

Learn about the Sounds at www.soundblends.com

Blend Sounds to Make Words

Blend Sounds to say Words...

Words

c a t

h o t

s a t

Say each Sound

Blend Sounds to say Words

Learn how to Blend Sounds at www.soundblends.com

Blend Sounds to say Words...

Sam Cat sat.

Blend Sounds to say Words

Read the Story!

Learn how to Read at www.soundblends.com

Letter Groups and Sight Words

Seeing Letter Groups...

Sound

Letter groups are used for 1 Sound

Light gray font with tight spacing

Sight Words use a Bold Gray Font...

to   a   of   the   was   I   are

The very few Sight Words are shown in a special font

Dark gray bold font with tight spacing

Learn about the Letter Groups at www.soundblends.com

Words with Syllables

Syllables use Chunks of Blended Sounds

Extra Space between Chunks

ca mel

⇧

First blend the Chunks

ca = c + a

mel = m + e + l

Combine the Chunks to make the Word!

Sounds and Letters in this Book

Hint: Don't use letter names! Use the sounds!

Vowel Sounds

a   as in   **an**   = **a** + n

e   as in   **egg**   = **e** + gg

i   as in   **in**   = **i** + n

o   as in   **off**   = **o** + ff

u   as in   **up**   = **u** + p

ay, ai   as in   **say**   = s   + **ay**

ee, ee   as in   see   = s + **ee**

ie, igh   as in   **sigh**   = s   + **igh**

oa, oe   as in   **oak**   = **oa** + k

ur, ir, er, urr   as in   sir   = s + **ir**

oy, oi   as in   **toy**   = t + **oy**

ow, ou   as in   **cow**   = c + **ow**

ar   as in   **car**   = c   + **ar**

ew, ue, oo   as in   coo   = c + **oo**

Sounds and Letters in this Book

Hint: Don't use letter names! Use the sounds!

Consonant Sounds

b, B, bb	as in **bed**	s, S, ss, se	as in **sit**
c, C, cc, k, K, ck	as in **cat**	t, T, tt	as in **tan**
d, D, dd	as in **dog**	v, V	as in **van**
f, F, ff	as in **fog**	w, W, wh	as in **win**
g, G, gg	as in **gorilla**	x, X	as in **fox**
h, H	as in **hat**	y, Y	as in **yell**
j, J	as in **jet**	z, Z, zz, ze	as in **zip**
l, L, ll	as in **lid**	th, Th	as in **that**
m, M, mm	as in **man**	sh, Sh	as in **ship**
n, N, nn	as in **nod**	ch, Ch, tch	as in **chip**
p, P, pp	as in **pan**	ng	as in **sing**
r, R	as in **rat**		

Sight Words

A   a   I   of   to   the   was   are

The **SoundBlendS** Pal

Snail presents...

The Fox and the Snail

Sounds

ai   ay   ch   tch

sh   th   ck   ll   gg

ss   zz

a   e   i   o   u

b   c   d   f   g   h

j   k   l   m   n   p

r   s   t   v   w   x

z

Words

gray   snail

play   way

rain   trail

stays   clay

nail   afraid

a   to   I

of   the   was

It is Sunday and a gray snail sits on a rock next to a trail. It is a gray day with gusts of wind.

Rain begins to drop on the snail. The rain splashes the dust on the trail and mixes into a thick clay mud.

A red fox jogs up the trail and spots the snail. The fox thinks that it is fun to play in a bad way.

The fox thinks that it is fun to kick snails. The red fox jumps onto the rock.

Then, the fox kicks the gray snail. The snail lands in the mud with a thud.

The thick mud gets on his shell. Then, the snail is afraid. The snail yells, "Stop, Fox, stop!

This is not **the** way **to** play. I am not big but I can still help with big problems."

The red fox scoffs
and tells the snail,
"A snail? A snail is
frail and can not
help a big fox.

A snail is not helpful." The snail tells the fox, "Just ask and I will help."

The fox stops and thinks. Then, **the** fox tells **the** snail, "Well, I will stop, but I expect help if I ask."

With that, the fox dashes off. Then, the snail inches up a stump. Wet mud is stuck to his shell.

The snail rubs the mud off and gets to the top of the stump. The snail rests until the next day.

At sunup, the snail gets up. His plan is to get to a pumpkin patch next to a chicken ranch.

The snail inches off the stump and gets on his way. The trail is still wet and **the** clay mud is thick.

The snail stays on the soft grass next to the trail. Then, the snail gets to the pumpkin patch.

Then, **the** snail spots **the** fox and **the** fox is sad. **The** fox's tail is stuck on **a** thin nail.

The fox tugs and tugs at his tail, but it is still stuck on the nail. The red fox can not get away.

The snail inches next to the fox and yells up to him, "This is a big mess. I can help!"

The fox spots the snail and tells him that his tail is stuck up on a nail up on the top rail.

The gray snail gets himself up to the top of the rail next to the nail. The snail lifts his tail off the nail.

The fox gets away. The fox is glad **to** get his tail unstuck and off that thin black nail.

The fox tells him, "I will not kick snails. A snail is not big but a snail is helpful." The fox runs off.

The snail is glad to help. But, the snail is glad that the fox runs away and will not stop to play.

The End

The SoundBlendS Pal

Bee Presents...

Sam Seal and Pam Eel

Sounds

ee ea

ai ay tch ch sh th

a e i o u

b c ck d f ff

g gg h j k l ll

m n p r s ss

t v w x z zz

Words

sea gull   hears

cheers   green

beach   seaweed

sleep   eat

week   east

a   to   I   of

the   was

Sam Seal feels sad. Sam wishes **to** play, but his pals went away on **a** trip. Sam misses his pals.

Sam Seal swims **to** a rock and sees **a** sea gull. "Sea gull, I wish **to** play with **a** pal. I wish **to** play swim and seek."

The gray sea gull gulps a shrimp in his beak and tells him, "I am a sea gull and can not swim."

With that, the sea gull sets off. Sam Seal is still sad and glum. Just then, Sam Seal hears a splash.

Next to the rock swims a green eel. The green eel swims up to Sam Seal and tells him, "I am Pam Eel.

I can play swim and seek." Then, Sam Seal cheers, "I think that is fun! Let us play next to the beach."

Sam Seal and Pam Eel swim across **the** sea **to** **the** beach. Near **the** beach, Sam Seal stops.

Sam Seal tells Pam Eel, "I will wait near **the** beach and not peek. But, let's not swim past **the** big rocks."

Pam Eel grins, nods and swims past the seaweed. Near the rocks, Pam Eel slips into a crack in the biggest rock.

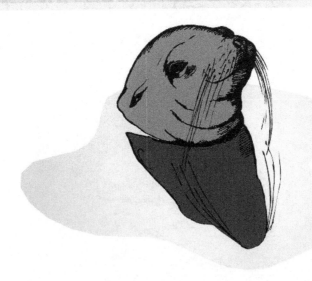

Sam Seal waits at **the** beach and then leaps into **to** **the** sea **to** seek his pal, Pam Eel.

Sam Seal swims to the seaweed but can not see Pam Eel. Pam Eel is not in the seaweed.

Then, Sam Seal swims back **to the** beach, but can not see Pam Eel. Pam Eel is not at **the** beach.

Sam Seal swims to the rocks and sees a green tail in a crack in the biggest rock.

Sam thinks that tail is Pam Eel. Sam Seal swims **to** tag that green tail. Sam Seal screams, "Tag!"

Pam Eel grins, swims up and tells him, "I am it." Pam Eel and Sam Seal swim back to the beach.

Just as Pam Eel nears the beach, a crab pops up. The crab stops Sam Seal and Pam Eel.

The crab tells them, "I need help. I just went to see a sunken ship on the reef.

On **the** ship is a big chest that has lots **of** shells. I need **to** fetch that big chest and get it in**to** that shed on **the** beach.

I wish **to** craft a model ship with **the** shells and play with it. **The** ship will need lots and lots **of** shells."

Sam Seal tells **the** crab, "If it is big, I can help drag **the** chest **to the** beach. I am not weak." Sam Seal grins.

Pam Eel tells the crab, "I will get strands of seaweed to help us drag the chest. Pam Eel gets the seaweed.

Then, Sam, Pam and the crab swim to the sunken ship. Pam Eel straps the seaweed to the chest.

Sam Seal drags the chest up to the beach. Sam Seal drags the chest into the shed. The crab is glad.

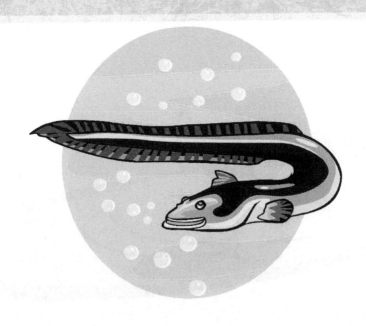

Sam Seal and Pam Eel swim in **the** sea. Sam Seal splashes Pam Eel with his tail. Pam Eel grins and splashes back.

Sam Seal tells Pam Eel, "This is fun, but I need **to** eat and sleep. Let's play next week."

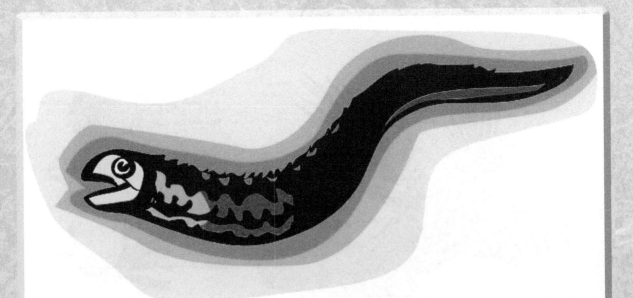

Pam Eel grins and tells Sam Seal, "I had lots of fun today. Let us meet at the beach next week."

Then, Sam Seal and Pam Eel swim off **to the** east. **The** sun sets. Sam Seal feels that this **was a** fantastic day.

The End

The SoundBlendS Pal

Goat Presents ...

The Picnic

Sounds

oa   oe   ee   ea   ai   ay

a   e   i   o   u

tch   ch   sh   th

b   bb   c   ck   d   dd

f   ff   g   gg   h   j   k

l   ll   m   n   p   r

s   ss   t   tt   v

w   x   z   zz

Words

goes	toast
soap	toe
road	croaks
hoe	moan
roasted	foam
goat	toad
oak	boats

a   to   I   of   was   the

It is Sunday. Jill Toad is in **the** kitchen. Jill Toad has plans **to** picnic with Joe Goat at Green Oak Pond. Jill Toad is fond **of** picnics at **the** pond.

It is fun to see the kids play at the pond. Kids swim, sail boats and catch fish. The best spot to picnic at the pond is near a swift stream that runs into the pond.

Jill Toad gets a basket and sets it on an oak bench. Then, Jill Toad gets roasted yams and sets it in the basket. Jill fills a canteen with milk to pack into the basket.

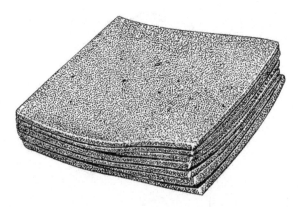

Jill Toad goes to the cabinet to get cloth napkins to pack in the basket. Jill Toad sees lots of gray dust on the napkins. Jill Toad gets a pail to clean them in.

Jill Toad fills the pail with soap and drops the cloth napkins into it. Jill swishes the napkins in the pail and the soap begins to foam. The foam feels soft on Jill's skin.

Just then, Jill Toad hears **a** moan. Then, Jill Toad hears **a** groan. Jill runs **to** see if it is Joe Goat. It is Joe Goat on **the** road. Joe Goat limps up **to** **the** steps and sits on them.

Joe Goat groans, "Jill, I got a cut." Jill Toad croaks, "Joe, is it a bad cut?" Joe Goat nods, "Yes." A bad cut on his left toe bleeds onto the steps next to Joe Goat.

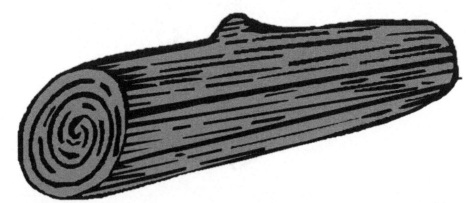

Then, Joe Goat tells Jill, "I was on the road near the oak tree at the top of the hill, I spotted a big log that lay across the road. I felt as if I had to get the log off the road.

As I lifted the log up, I am afraid to say that I did not see the big nail beneath the log. As I lifted the log off the road, that nail cut this back left toe."

With that, Joe Goat grabs his back left toe **to** let Jill see his cut. Then, Jill Toad pats his leg, "I can help. Sit still and I will get **a** wet cloth **to** clean up **the** cut on **the** bad toe."

Jill Toad goes in **the** kitchen and grabs a wet cloth napkin. Then, Jill goes back **to** Joe Goat and cleans off his toe. Then, Jill Toad goes back **to the** kitchen **to** get a band-aid.

The band-aid will stop his bleed and keep the cut clean. Jill patches up the cut with the band-aid. Jill Toad then croaks, "That seems to fix the cut." Jill grins at Joe Goat.

Joe Goat still seems sad and tells Jill, "I am sad. I can not hop **to** **the** stream next **to** Green Oak Pond with **a** bad toe. And it is such **a** fantastic day **to** picnic."

Jill Toad grins and croaks, "I can set up the picnic on the grass next to the beech tree." Then, Joe Goat grins, "That is a fantastic plan. A picnic beneath the beech tree is fun."

Jill Toad goes into the kitchen and gets a red and tan picnic sheet and the basket with the treats. Jill hops off the steps and onto the grass. Then, Jill goes up the hill to the beech tree.

Jill Toad lays **the** sheet next **to the** beech tree and sets **the** basket on it. Then, Jill sees Jon Rabbit next **to** his beans and peas. Jon Rabbit has **a** hoe in his hand **to** clear **the** weeds.

Jill Toad croaks to Jon Rabbit, "Jon, I need help. Joe Goat has a cut on his toe and can not help with the set up. I need to set up a picnic bench next to the beech tree."

Jon Rabbit tells Jill Toad, "I can help. I will get the picnic bench and set it up near the tree." With that, the rabbit leans his hoe onto a box and goes to get a bench.

Jill Toad goes back and helps Joe Goat hop **to the** beech tree. Joe Goat leans on Jill Toad and limps across **the** green grass and up **the** hill **to the** beech tree.

Jon Rabbit sets up the bench next to the basket and Joe Goat sits on it. Jill Toad grins at Jon Rabbit and hugs him. Jon Rabbit goes back to his peas and beans and picks up his hoe.

Jill Toad sets up **the** picnic lunch **to** eat next **to the** beech tree. Jill Toad hands him a toast with roasted yams on it. Joe Goat tells Jill Toad that this is a fun picnic lunch.

The End

The **SoundBlendS** Pal

Bird presents ...

Kersten and the Cat

Sounds

ur   ir   er   urr

oa   oe   ee   ea   ai   ay

a   e   i   o   u

tch   ch   sh   th

b   bb   c   ck   d   dd

f   ff   g   gg   h   j   k

l   ll   m   n   p   r   s   ss

t   tt   v   w   x   z   zz

Words

Thursday	bird
chirp	her
crackers	terrific
fur	purr
third	butter
first	girl

a   to   I   of   was

the   A

It is Thursday and a bird sits in her nest. Her nest is up at the top of a birch tree. This bird is Kersten Bird. Kersten is a gray bird with a red throat, a tan beak and green feet.

Kersten gets up and begins **to** chirp and clean up her nest at **the** top **of** that birch tree. It is **a** clear day with lots of sun. Kersten is glad.

Today, her sister, Shirl Bird, is **to** visit, sip tea and eat lunch with her. Kersten gets **a** dish **to** set **the** crackers, toast and peanut butter on. Then, Kersten gets **a** tea pot and fills it.

Kersten plugs **the** tea pot in **to** heat it up. Kersten goes **to** her kitchen and gets **a** soft green cloth. After Kersten lays **the** cloth on her bench, Shirl lands on **the** rim **of** her nest.

Kersten greets Shirl with a big hug. Shirl is glad to see her sister. It is fun to eat lunch in her sister's nest. Shirl helps Kersten set the cups and dishes on the bench.

Kersten gets the tea and sets it on her bench. The sisters then sit next to the bench and begin to eat. Shirl smears the peanut butter on a cracker and snaps it up in her beak.

Then, Shirl sips her hot tea. Shirl chirps **to** Kersten, "This tea is terrific. It is fun **to** lunch on tea and crackers. I am fond **of** toast as well."

Kersten grins and chirps, "Shirl, this is wonderful **to** eat lunch with such **a** fun sister." After lunch, Shirl helps Kersten clean up **the** cups and dishes.

Then, Shirl soars off **to**
her nest. Under
Kersten's nest, **a** cat
sneaks in **the** wet,
green grass. Kersten
can not see **the** cat.
The lean cat creeps
under **the** birch tree.

The cat's fur has dirt in it, and **the** cat has not had **a** meal in three days. The cat needs **to** eat. The cat sees **the** crackers and toast and smells **the** peanut butter in Kersten's nest.

The cat stops and purrs, "Bird, bird, can I get that cracker with a bit of peanut butter on it?" It is a shock to hear the cat's purr. Kersten Bird has never trusted cats.

Kersten leans on the rim of her nest and spots the cat under the tree. Kersten did not wish to help the cat. But, Kersten can see that the cat is lean and needs to eat.

Kersten Bird chirps **to** **the** cat, "Will three crackers with peanut butter help?" **The** cat grins and purrs, "Yes." Kersten Bird smears peanut butter on three crackers.

Then, Kersten yells, "Catch!" and tosses them **to the** cat. The cat snatches up **the** crackers in **a** flash. **The** cat purrs, "Can I get another cracker with peanut butter?"

Then, Kersten Bird feels fear. Kersten is afraid that **the** cat will not stop. Kersten Bird chirps **to the** cat, "That is it, cat. I need **to** keep **the** rest **to** eat at supper."

The cat is not glad. The cat gets mad. The cat jumps up on the first branch in the birch tree and then to the third branch. Then, the cat jumps up to Kersten's nest.

In a flash, Kersten Bird packs up the crackers, the toast and the peanut butter and flees. Kersten goes east and sees a girl with wonderful black curls and a sweet grin.

Then, Kersten has a terrific plan to keep the cat away. Kersten stops and tells the girl, "Girl, I need help with a mean cat. I need a silver bell to attach to the cat's tail.

At first I was helpful. I let her eat three crackers, but that cat did not stop. If I can hear that silver bell on the cat's tail, then I can tell if the cat will attack.

The girl with the wonderful black curls grins and tells the bird, "I can get a bell with a red ribbon to attach to her neck." The girl goes to her kitchen and gets the silver bell.

Then, **the** girl goes with Kersten back **to** her nest. The cat is stuck up in **the** nest. Kersten soars up **to** her nest and attaches **the** bell **to** the cat's neck.

Then, the cat is sad. The cat begins to sob and wail. The girl sees that the cat needs a pal and goes up to get her. The girl pets the cat and the cat begins to purr.

Perhaps **the** cat is not mean, but just needs **to** eat. **The** girl lifts up **the** cat and lugs her back **to** her kitchen **to** feed her. Kersten is glad that **the** cat has left and will not bother her.

The End

The **SoundBlendS** Pal

Raccoon presents ...

Sue at the Zoo

Sounds

ue   oo   ew

ur   ir   er   urr   oa   oe

ee   ea   ai   ay

a   e   i   o   u

tch   ch   sh   th

b   bb   c   cc   ck   d   dd   f

ff   g   gg   h   j   k   l

ll   m   n   p   r   s   ss   t

tt   v   w   x   z   zz

Words

Tuesday	zoo
smooth	new
scooter	blue
rooster	chews
raccoon	true
blew	balloon

a   to   I   of   was

the   A

It is Tuesday. Today is **the** day that Sue and her pal, Lee, plan **to** visit **the** zoo. Sue gets up and gets on her green top and blue jeans. Sue's dog, Tazz, licks her on her chin.

Sue gets a brush and brushes her curls into a smooth pigtail. Then, Sue gets a toothbrush and floss to clean her teeth. Sue cleans up her room and then goes to get food.

Sue runs into the kitchen to eat. Sue's dad greets her with a big hug. Then, Sue's dad gets a blue dish and sets it next to Sue. Sue fills a blue cup with tea and sets it next to her dish.

Sue's mom cuts up a peach and hands it **to** Sue. Sue's dad flips **the** French toast on**to** Sue's dish. Sue gets herself **a** glass **of** milk and sits on **a** stool **to** eat.

Sue eats **the** peach and French toast with butter. Then, Sue sips her milk and tea. Sue cleans up her dishes and sets them in **the** sink. Just then, Sue hears **a** bell. Sue goes **to** let Lee in.

Lee is on the front steps. Lee greets Sue with a big hug. Lee has a blue scooter and a helmet. Lee's helmet is blue, too. Lee sits on a stool and waits until Sue finishes her clean-up.

Sue's dad cleans up the pan in the kitchen sink and then gets on his coat. Sue's mom kisses her and goes back to the kitchen to finish the clean-up. Sue gets her new blue scooter.

Sue got her scooter on her tenth birthday last week. After Sue gets her helmet on, **the** girls and Sue's dad set off. **The** zoo is ten blocks away.

It is a terrific day to visit the zoo. The day is clear, and the sun is not too hot. The gusts of wind cool the girls' cheeks. But, the wind is not too much to bother them.

Sue's dad has **to** jog **to** keep up with **the** girls on **the** scooters. **The** girls must cross **a** big road **to** get **to** **the** zoo. At **the** zoo, **the** girls lock up **the** scooters under **a** big oak tree.

Sue's dad gets the tickets. In the zoo, the girls skip on the trail to the bird exhibit. Sue's dad goes with them. The room with the bird exhibit has lots of different birds.

A net covers the top of the room to keep the birds in. The first bird that Sue sees is a black loon. The loon swims on a cool, smooth pond. The loon catches a fish to eat.

A green and gray toad croaks at the loon as it sits in the dirt next to the pond. Lee sees a rooster peck and scratch at bugs in the wet grass.

The rooster is black with patches **of** tan on its chest and back. Next **to the** rooster is **a** mother hen with her brood of new chicks. Sue sees **a** bird feeder.

Sue lifts the latch on the bird feeder and gets a handful of grain to toss to the birds. A blue bird lands on a branch and chirps. Sue grins and tosses a bit of grain on the grass.

The blue bird swoops off the branch and snatches up the bits of grain. After the bird exhibit, the girls and Sue's dad see a panda. The panda sits and chews on bamboo.

Sue asks her dad if it is true that pandas eat just bamboo. Sue's dad tells her that pandas prefer **to** eat just bamboo but can eat other food, such as fish and mushrooms, too.

In the next exhibit, Sue sees a raccoon as it scoots on an oak branch up near the roof. The raccoon scampers off the branch and onto a box hidden up in the tree.

The raccoon has black and gray fur. The raccoon sees a bit of food that the zoo keepers had left in his dish. The raccoon snatches up his food and chews on it.

At that, Sue asks her dad **to** get lunch. Sue's dad sees **a** clock, and it is noon. Sue's dad sees **a** hot dog booth and goes **to** get food. Sue's dad gets **the** girls hot dogs **to** eat.

Next to the hot dog booth stands a man with lots of balloons. As the girls began to chew the hot dogs, the man attaches another balloon to his stand. The balloon is blue.

Sue grins at her dad and asks him **to** get a balloon.   Sue's dad grins back at Sue and gets up.   Sue's dad goes **to** **the** balloon man and gets six blue balloons.

Sue's dad hands three balloons to each girl. The girls grab the balloons and hug Sue's dad. Then, the girls skip to the zoo exit to get the scooters. Sue gets her helmet on.

Lee gets her helmet on, too. The wind gusts up, and Sue grins. Sue gets a balloon and lets it float away. Then, Sue's dad attaches the rest of the balloons to the girls' scooters.

Sue hugs her dad and tells him, "This is fantastic, Dad. I had a fun visit to the zoo." Sue's dad hugs her and tells her, "I had a fun visit, too."

The End

The **SoundBlendS** Pal

Owl presents ...

Ben the Groundhog

Sounds

ow   ou

ue   oo   ew   ur   ir   er   urr

oa   oe   ee   ea   ai   ay

a   e   i   o   u

tch   ch   sh   th

b   bb   c   cc   ck   d   dd   f

ff   g   gg   h   j   k   l   ll

m   mm   n   p   r   s   ss

t   tt   v   w   x   z   zz

Words

brown

flowers

down

owl

without

groundhog

out

around

cow

allows

crown

loud

a   to   I   of   was

the

Today is Saturday. It is Ben's birthday. Ben is six. Ben is asleep in his bed. Ben is a groundhog with brown fur. Ben and his mom sleep in a snug den underground.

His den is under a mound of dirt up on a hill. At sunup, Ben's mom gets him up and out of bed. Ben picks out a brown shirt with black pants and gets them on.

Then, Ben goes out to the kitchen and sits on a stool. Ben's mom goes with him and gets out a dish to set on the counter. Ben's mom sets seeds and nuts on the dish.

As Ben eats his meal, Ben's mom sets a big box on the counter. Ben grins. In the box is a hat, a new blue coat and soft brown boots. Ben is glad and hugs his mom.

Ben gets on his new coat, boots and hat. Ben asks his mom, "Mom, may I play out on the grass?" Ben's mom grins and tells him, "First, clean up and then play."

Ben **the** groundhog grins and runs back **to** his room. Ben cleans his room and brushes his teeth. Then, Ben goes back **to** see his mom. Ben asks his mom, "May I play, now?"

Ben's mom grins and tells him, "Yes, but stay on the patch of grass near the den." Ben goes out. It is summer. The grass is now brown and blends well with Ben's fur.

Ben runs around and leaps off a mound of dirt near his den. Ben spins around and lands with a loud thud in the dirt. Ben stops and sees a cow.

The cow stands under an oak tree and chews grass. Ben goes up to the cow and asks to play with her. The cow stops and tells Ben," It is too hot to play."

Then, **the** cow goes back **to** her grass. Ben hops and bounds back **to** his den. Near his den is **a** patch **of** flowers. His pal, Roxee Rabbit, sits in **the** flowers. Roxee is fun **to** play with.

Ben asks Rox ee **to** play with him. Rox ee grins and tells Ben, "It is fun **to** pick fresh flowers and braid them in**to** crowns. How about that?" Ben nods and sits down next **to** Rox ee.

Ben begins to pick flowers. Ben braids the flowers into a crown and hands it to Roxee. Roxee grins and tells Ben that her mom expects her back at noon. Roxee hops off.

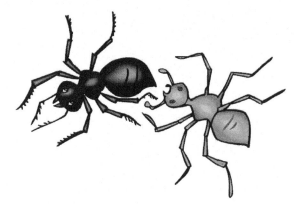

Ben feels restless and begins to dig in the dirt to catch bugs. Ben catches ten ants and a pill bug and dumps them into his front pocket. Ben sits down.

It is noon, now, and it is hot out in the sun. Down the hill and under an oak tree is a cool creek. With it this hot, Ben thinks that it will feel fantastic to swim in that creek.

Ben's mom never allows him **to** swim without an adult. But Ben feels hot. Ben sees that dirt has gotten on his new coat and boots. Ben thinks that **a** cool swim will clean off **the** dirt.

Ben sneaks down **the** hill **to** **the** cool creek under **the** oak tree. Ben stops under **the** tree and sits down. Just then, Ben sees **a** big owl up in **the** oak tree. Owls can catch and eat groundhogs.

Ben feels afraid. Ben jumps up and runs back **to** his den. **The** owl sees Ben and soars after him. Ben lets out **a** loud scream. Ben's mom pops out **of the** den and picks up **a** rock.

Just as the owl is about to grab Ben, Ben's mom gets to him and hurls the rock at the owl. The rock hits the owl's leg. The owl screams, flinches and then goes away.

Ben begins to sob and wail. Ben's mom hugs him and leads him back to the den. Back in his snug den, Ben sits down on a stool in the kitchen.

Ben sobs **to** his mom, "Mom, **I** **was** afraid. That owl just about got..." Sad and upset, Ben stops. Then, Ben goes on **to** tell his mom, "**I** **was** hot, Mom.

I sat in dirt, and it got on **the** new coat and boots. I went **to** swim in **the** creek **to** clean them off and cool down. I will not sneak off **to** swim in that creek, ever! That **was a** bad plan."

His mom frowns and tells him, "Ben, it is fun **to** swim in that cool creek on **a** hot day such as this. But, it is much better **to** swim **to**gether." Ben nods.

His mom hugs him and Ben feels much, much better. Ben feels snug in his den and finishes the rest of his birthday with his mom in his snug den under the hill.

The SoundBlendS Pal

Dog presents ...

Pam and Her Dog, Kie

Sounds

igh   ie   ow   ou

ue oo ew ur ir er urr

oa oe   ee ea ai ay

a e i o u

tch   ch   sh   th

b bb c cc ck d dd f

ff g gg h j k l ll

m mm n p r s ss t

tt v w x z zz

Words

right	fried
light	ties
pie	bright
tries	high
higher	fight
sighs	might

a   to   I   of

was   the

Today is Tuesday. Pam gets up and out of bed. It is summer and the bright light from the sun's rays stream into her room. Pam's dog, bounds into her room and jumps right up on her.

Kie licks Pam's cheek and lies down next to her. Pam pets Kie's soft brown fur. Pam is fond of her dog, Kie. Kie twitches his ears at her. Pam can tell that Kie wishes to eat right now.

Pam goes **to the** kitchen and gets out Kie's food. Kie chews his food with glee. Pam sees her mom and greets her with a hug. Pam's mom gets out a blue dish and sets a fried egg on it.

Pam sits on a stool and eats her fried egg. Pam thinks about her plans. Today, Pam plans to visit her pal, Val. Pam tells her mom, "Mom, I had plans to visit Val, today."

Pam's mom tells her, "Sounds fun." Pam goes **to** her room and picks out **a** bright green shirt with blue jeans. Then, Pam goes in**to** **the** bathroom, turns on **a** light and brushes her teeth.

Pam goes **to** get Kie's leash and attaches it **to** him. Pam goes **to** get her scooter and helmet. Pam attaches her helmet under her chin and ties Kie's leash **to** her scooter.

Then, Pam and Kie set off. It is a bright and clear day. Not a cloud in sight. Pam turns right at the stop light and goes ten blocks. Val is out on her front steps. Val sees Pam.

Pam ties up Kie under the birch tree. Val gets Kie a dish with a cool drink. The girls see Val's mom. Val's mom is a vet. Val's mom has to help out at the clinic today.

Val's mom tells her, "Val, tell Dad that I will finish at noon today." Val agrees to tell her Dad. Then, Val's mom gets her lab coat, hops in her van and goes to the clinic.

Pam asks Val, "May I get a snack?" Val grins at Pam and tells her, "Mom got a peach pie, yesterday. How about that?" Pam grins, "That sounds wonderful."

Val goes into the kitchen to get the peach pie. It is up high on a shelf. Val drags a stool next to the peach pie. Val gets up on the stool and tries to reach the pie. It is too high.

Val gets up on her toes and tries **to** reach **the** pie. It is still too high. Val sighs, "Pam, I tried but I can not reach **the** pie." Pam grins and tells Val, "I can reach higher. Let's see if I can reach it."

Val gets off **the** stool and Pam gets on it. Pam stands on **the** tips **of** her toes. Pam reaches and gets **the** peach pie. Then, Pam gets down with **the** pie and sets it on **the** counter.

Val gets out the dishes and spoons. Val cuts up the pie and sets Pam's on her dish. Then, Val sets hers on another dish. Pam gets the milk out and fills the girls' glasses.

Pam sighs, "This pie is a fantastic snack." After snack, the girls clean up. Then, the girls skip out the back, across the deck and then see that Val's dad is in the tool shed.

The girls skip to the tool shed. Val's dad gets out a hammer and nails to help fix the back deck. Val tells her dad, "Dad, Mom is at the clinic today and will finish at noon."

Val's dad stops next to the girls and asks, "Val, how about a visit to the clinic today? I think that it might teach Pam about how vets help pets to get better."

Val grins, "That is a wonderful plan. How about it, Pam?" Pam grins and tells Val, "That sounds fantastic. Let's get Kie and visit the clinic, now."

Pam goes out **to** get Kie and Val gets her scooter and helmet. Pam ties Kie's leash **to** her scooter and **the** girls set off. It is ten blocks **to the** vet's clinic.

Pam keeps **a** tight leash on Kie **to** keep him away from **the** big trucks. The girls need **to** cross **a** big road. At **the** stop light, Pam presses **the** button and **the** girls wait until **the** light turns green.

The girls cross the road and turn right onto Oak Street, just past the stop light. The clinic is down on the right at the end of the street. At the clinic, the girls lock up the scooters.

Pam unties Kie. Val goes **to** see if her mom can let them visit with her **to**day. Pam goes and waits in **the** clinic with Kie. Three cats and six dogs wait next **to** Kie and Pam.

Val sees her mom in **the** back. Val tells her mom that Pam is in **the** front with Kie. Val goes with her mom **to** get Pam. Just then, Kie steps back and on**to** **the** tail **of** a hurt cat.

The cat screams and hisses. The cat leaps on Kie and scratches his ear. Kie howls as his ear begins to bleed. The girl with the cat tries to grab her, but the cat hisses at her, too.

Val's mom tries **to** stop **the** fight. Val's mom lifts **the** cat off **of** Kie and hands her back **to** **the** girl. Then, Val's mom leads Kie back **to a** room and lifts him on**to a** high counter.

It is just a slight cut and three stitches will patch it up. Pam hugs Kie as Val's mom stitches up his ear. Pam tells Val's mom, "I got to see firsthand how vets can help dogs."

Val's mom grins at Pam and asks her, "How about a visit around the rest of the clinic to see other cats and dogs that need help?" Pam grins and tells her, "That sounds fantastic."

The End

The SoundBlends Pal

Oyster presents ...

Roy and His Toy

Sounds

oy   oi   igh   ie   ow   ou

ue   oo   ew   ur   ir   er   urr

oa   oe   ee   ea   ai   ay

a   e   i   o   u

tch   ch   sh   th

b   bb   c   cc   ck   d   dd   f

ff   g   gg   h   j   k   l   ll

m   mm   n   p   pp   r   s   ss

t   tt   v   w   x   z   zz

Words

boil   oil

toy   coins

enjoys   spoil

moist   avoid

poison   joy

hoists   ointment

boy   oinks

a   to   I   of   was   the

Today is Tuesday. It is the first day of Roy's summer holiday. Roy gets up and gets out his blue jeans and red shirt. Roy's dog, Spot, bounds into his room and licks his chin.

Roy grins and pets his dog. Spot has a brown spot on his right cheek. Roy gets his pants and shirt on and goes to the bathroom to brush his teeth. Then, Roy goes to the kitchen to eat.

Roy's mom and dad hug him. Roy's dad brews three cups of tea and hands Roy's to him. Roy adds milk to his hot tea and begins to sip it. Roy's mom sets an egg in a hot pot to boil.

Roy's dad gets out a pan, oils it, and begins to heat it up. Then, Roy's dad tosses ham in the hot oil and fries it until it is crisp and brown. It smells terrific. Roy gets out a blue dish.

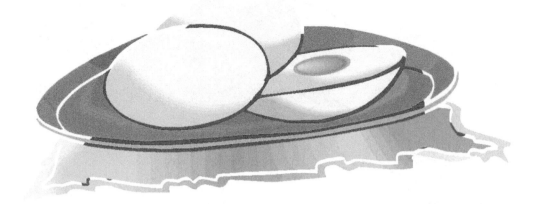

After the egg heats up to a soft boil, Roy's mom peels the shell off the egg. Then, his mom cuts it up with a silver spoon. Roy sits down and his mom loads his dish with the fried ham and egg.

After Roy eats his egg, Spot tugs at his pant leg. Roy rubs Spot's ears and gets him his dog food. Spot chews his food with glee. Roy cleans up his dish, his spoon and tea cup.

Then, Roy asks his mom, "Mom, may I play down at the pond today with Spot?" Roy's mom grins and tells him, "That sounds fun. Just stay on the right path and keep Spot on his leash."

Roy grins and runs to get his new toy sailboat. His dad had given him the new toy on his birthday last May. Now that it is his summer holiday, Roy can sail it on the pond.

Roy gets his backpack and packs his new toy, **a** towel, and **a** snack **to** eat at **the** pond. Roy gets out three copper coins and packs them in his backpack, too.

Down the road and on the way to the pond is a deep well. The well has a bucket tied to a stick. The bucket can drop down into the pool at the bottom of the well.

Now and then, kids will pass the well and stop to toss coins in it. As the coins disappear down into the well, kids can express a wish and dream that it might happen.

Roy thinks that it is fun to toss **the** coins down **the** well and dream that his wish might happen. His backpack is now crowded with **the** stuff Roy needs at **the** pond. Roy zips up his backpack.

Roy gets Spot's leash and attaches it to him. The boy and his dog set off. Roy jumps off the cabin steps and onto the soft grass. Spot leaps after him.

Roy enjoys his visits to the pond. Spot enjoys them, too. It is a bright summer day and the sun is hot. Thin clouds float up high, but it is clear that rain will not spoil this day.

Roy and Spot set off down the path to the pond. The path is next to a big road. Roy keeps Spot on a tight leash and tries to avoid the big trucks that thunder past them on the road.

On the way, Roy sees a big stick next to the path. Roy picks up the stick and points it at a brown cow. Roy moos at the cow. The cow sees that Roy is just a boy and goes back to her grass.

Then, Roy skips off down the path with Spot. The path turns right near a sluggish creek. Roy turns right and skips down the path. Then, Roy sees the well next to the path and stops.

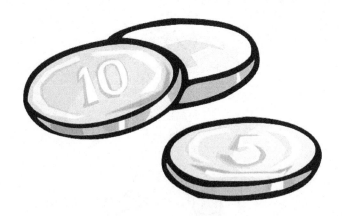

Roy unzips his backpack and gets out his three copper coins. Roy tries **to** think **of** **a** terrific wish. Then, Roy tosses his three copper coins in**to** **the** well and murmurs **a** wish.

Roy wishes that his summer holiday will never end. Roy hears a splash deep down in the well. Roy grins. Perhaps his wish will never happen, but it is still fun to dream.

A creek runs near **the** well and Roy sees **a** big oak tree next **to** it. Roy sits down under **the** oak tree. Six pigs grunt and root at bugs in **the** moist soil next **to** **the** creek.

Roy oinks at the pigs. Roy stands up. Roy tries to get the pigs to play with him and Spot, but the pigs' interest is in the bugs in the mud, not in the boy.

Roy tosses his stick across the creek. Then, Roy points at the stick and tells Spot, "Fetch the stick, Spot." Roy unlatches his leash and Spot leaps into the creek.

Spot splashes across the creek and snatches up the stick. Spot then runs back to Roy. Spot drops the stick and leaps up on him. With a loud thump, Roy lands in the mud.

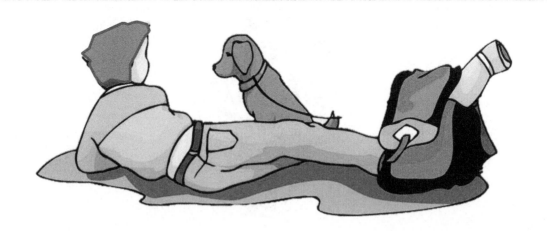

Spot lands on top **of** him. Roy grins at Spot and rubs his ears. Then, Roy gets up and cleans **the** mud off his backpack and pants. Roy gets Spot's leash back on and sets off up **the** creek.

The pond is up the creek a bit. Roy keeps Spot next to him and out of the poison oak. Last summer, Spot had gotten in the poison oak and had gotten a bad itch that had lasted three days.

Roy had gotten an ointment that helps lessen **the** itch. But still, Roy did not wish that **to** happen this summer, too. Up **the** creek at **the** pond, Roy gets out **a** snack **to** eat.

Spot goes down to the pond and laps up a cool drink. Roy gets out his new toy sailboat. It has blue sails. Roy hoists up the sails and sets it in the pond.

A puff of wind fills the blue sails, and the toy boat sets off across the pond. Roy's toy gets stuck in the reeds. Roy kicks off his socks and boots and splashes in to get his sailboat.

The wet sand and mud in the pond feels cool to his hot toes. Spot leaps into the pond and splashes Roy. Roy gets wet. Roy grabs his toy sailboat and gets out of the pond.

Roy sits on **the** sand and grins. Roy is wet from tip **to** toe. Roy gets **a** towel out **of** his backpack and dries off. Spot wags his tail and plops down next **to** Roy.

Roy hears a frog croak in the reeds next to the pond. Roy sees a bird as it soars up high into the clouds. Crickets chirp, and ducks swim on the pond.

The soft sounds of summer murmur in Roy's ears. Roy runs his hand in the wet sand. It feels cool on such a hot day. Roy thinks that it is true that summer is the best season.

Roy enjoys **the** free summer days, his dog and this first trip **to** his pond. Roy wishes that it will never end. Roy sits with Spot, his new toy, and enjoys his first real day **of** summer.

The End

The **SoundBlendS** Pal

S h a r k   p r e s e n t s   ...

The Farm Trip

Sounds

ar   se   ze   ve

oy   oi   igh   ie   ow   ou

ue   oo   ew   ur   ir   er   urr

oa   oe   ee   ea   ai   ay

a e i o u tch ch sh th

b bb c cc ck d f ff

g gg h j k l ll m

mm n nn p r s ss

t tt v w x z zz

Words

f ar m   fr ee ze

h ar n e ss   sn ee ze

b ar n y ar d   br ee ze

g ar d en er   h ou se

g i ve   g ee se

h a ve   l oo se

l ea ve s   h or se

are   a   to   I   of

was   the

Just as **the** first sun rays stream in**to** his room, Mark's alarm clock goes off. Mark hits **the** snooze bar and tries **to** block out **the** bright summer sun with his soft blue cover.

But Mark's dog, Barb, bounds in**to** his room and leaps on**to** his bed. Barb licks Mark's chin. Mark grins. If Barb is up then Mark will never get back **to** sleep. Mark gets up and out **of** his bed.

Mark grabs a bronze tee-shirt and blue jeans out of his closet. Barb jumps up on him to ask him to get her food to eat. Mark slips on gray flip-flops and shoos Barb out of his room.

Mark lives in a brown house with three big oak trees in his yard. The green leaves help keep his house cool on hot days such as this. It is still cool, but it will get much hotter in the afternoon.

Mark goes into the kitchen and gets out Barb's dog food and dish. Mark tells her to sit and wait. Barb sits and wags her tail. Then, Mark gives Barb her dish. His dog bolts down her food.

Then, Mark goes and sits on a stool next **to the** counter. Mark's mom and dad each give him **a** big hug. His dad tells Mark, "Mom and I have plans **to** visit Royal Creek Farm **to**day."

Mark grins. Mark enjoys his visits **to the** farm. The cows, **the** sheep, and **the** geese **are** fun **to** see. Mark tells his dad, "That sounds fantastic. **The** farm is such **a** fun spot **to** visit."

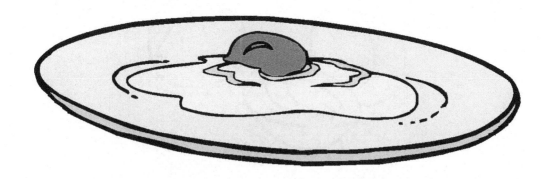

Mark's dad grins and tells him, "Terrific! Let's eat first and then set out after the clean-up." Mark's mom serves him a dish with fried eggs and ham on it.

Mark's dad cuts up a peach and sets it on Mark's dish, too. Barb finishes her food and sits next to Mark. Then, Mark's dad heats up a mug of milk and hands it to him.

Mark sips **the** hot milk and eats his meal. Mark then cleans up his dish and rinses out his mug. Then, Mark dashes back **to** his bathroom **to** brush his teeth. Mark's dog, Barb, goes with him.

Then, Mark goes back into the kitchen. Mark's dad packs up a picnic basket with sandwiches and boxes of milk. Mark's mom helps his dad pack up her car with the picnic basket.

Barb tries **to** get in **the** car. But, Mark tells Barb that dogs **are** not permitted at **the** farm. **The** farmers **are** afraid that dogs might frighten **the** farm animals. Barb barks at Mark.

Mark can tell that Barb wishes **to** visit **the** farm, too. Mark pets Barb's ears and tells her **to** wait in his room. Barb seems sad, but trots off **to** Mark's room.

Then, Mark goes out **to** wait in his mom's car. It is hot in her car, but **a** fresh breeze feels cool on his cheeks. His mom grabs her purse and locks **the** house.

Just after his dad gets in, his mom starts the car. His mom goes down the road and around a tight curve. At the stoplight, his mom turns right. Royal Creek Farm is not far.

Soon, Mark can see **the** farm up on **a** hill. The farm has **a** big red barn with "Royal Creek Farm" painted in big black letters. Mark's mom parks her car and gets out.

A big olive tree is next to the car. The breeze sweeps a dense cloud of pollen off the olive tree. The pollen drifts down. Olive tree pollen can trigger a sneeze. Mark sneezes.

Next to the farm is a park. The park has a pond that geese and ducks can swim in. It has lots of dirt trails that curve in between big oak and olive trees. And, it has a fun playground.

Mark's dad asks him, "After our visit to the farm, how about the three of us have a picnic lunch at the park?" Mark grins and tells his dad, "Fantastic, Dad! That sounds fun."

Mark starts **to** run up **the** trail. But, Mark's mom asks him **to** stay with them. Mark grins and stops **to** wait. Then, Mark gives his mom his hand **to** cross **the** street.

The trail goes up the hill to the farm. Mark, his mom, and his dad first see the barnyard with the chickens and sheep. The hens scratch at the dirt and peck at the bugs hidden in the grass.

The sheep chew grass under an oak tree. It is cool under the tree. The grass is thick and green. The sheep enjoy the fresh grass. Then, Mark goes up the hill farther to see the cows.

At the milk shed, a farmer ties up a cow to milk her. Then, the man starts to milk the cow. The fresh milk streams into the clean bucket. It is fun to see how farmers milk cows.

After the cows, Mark goes into the big red barn. In the barn is an exhibit about wool yarn. Mounds of wool sit in a big basket. The wool was cut off the sheep last March.

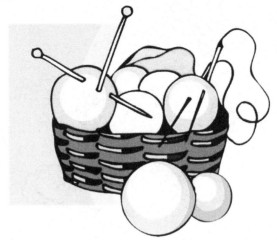

A man grabs out a handful of wool and cards it into thin strands. Then, the man twists the wool and coils it onto a yarn spool. Mark feels the wool yarn. It feels soft.

After that, Mark goes down the hill to see the goats. Mark leans on the top rail of the goat pen. The goat kids run loose and play. The goat does and bucks eat hay in the cool shed.

Mark sees a man approach the goat pen. The man has a goat cart and harness with him. The man goes in the pen and offers a big buck a treat. The buck snatches the treat out of his hand.

Then, the man attaches the harness to the big goat buck. Mark is interested in the goat and the cart. Mark asks the man, "That seems fun. May I help set up the cart?"

The man grins at Mark and tells him, "Yes. Get the cart, drag it into this goat pen and then turn it around. I will lead the goat between the shafts. Then, I will need help with the straps."

Mark grins and goes **to** get **the** goat cart. Mark gets **the** cart and drags it in**to** **the** goat pen. The kid goats **are** afraid **of** **the** cart noise and give him lots **of** room. Mark turns **the** cart around.

Then, the man leads the goat between the shafts and hands Mark the left part of the harness strap. The man tells him, "Tie that part of the strap onto the cart shaft."

Mark tries **to** loop **the** strap around but it slips off. Mark tells **the** man, "This is too hard. I can not get it. The strap is too loose and it will not stay on **the** shaft."

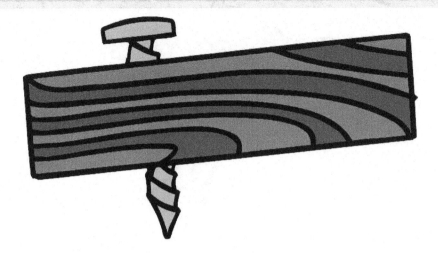

The man grins and tells Mark, "Loop it around that screw first and then tie it off." Mark sees the screw on the cart shaft, loops the strap around it and then ties it off.

Then, Mark goes around the cart and gets the other strap. This part of the harness needs to attach to the right shaft. Mark loops it around the right screw and then ties that strap off too.

The man grins and tells Mark, "Fantastic job with the harness!" Then, the man asks him, "As payment, how about a lift in the cart up the hill to the garden?

The gardener needs this cart now." Mark shouts, "Yes!" and gets in the cart. The garden is on top of the hill next to the big red barn. The man tugs on the harness to get started.

The goat starts to trot and leaves the pen. Mark's mom and dad stay in back of the cart as it goes up the hill. Mark thinks that it is fun to travel in a goat cart.

At **the** garden, **the** man stops **the** goat cart and Mark gets out. Mark grins. That **was** fun! **The** man then leads **the** cart **to** **a** shed next **to** **the** garden and starts **to** load it with bark.

The bark is to cover the paths in the garden and keep the weeds out. The garden has paths between the plants. The flowers are on the right, and the food plants are on the left.

A gardener hoes weeds near **the** radishes. **The** gardener grins and asks him, "As **a** treat, how about **a** bit **of** fresh radish?" Mark points at **a** green plant and asks, "Is that **a** radish?"

The gardener tugs at the green plant and out pops a red round radish. The gardener rinses the dirt off the radish and gives it to Mark. Mark crunches his teeth into the fresh radish.

It is crisp and Mark enjoys it. Mark turns and asks his mom, "Is it lunch, yet?" Mark's mom grins, "Yes. How about a picnic down at the park?"

Mark cheers and tells his mom, "That sounds fantastic." Mark goes back down the trail to the park with his mom. His dad goes out to the car to get the picnic lunch.

Down at the park, Mark's mom and dad set up the picnic lunch. It is now hot and the pond seems cool. Mark kicks off his flip-flops and goes into the pond. The geese and the ducks swim away.

Mark can feel **the** mud ooze between his toes. It feels terrific on his hot feet. Then, Mark goes back **to** clean and rinse off his hands and then eat lunch. **The** sandwiches and milk **are** fantastic.

Just after his sandwich, Mark sees a man with a cooler on a cart. The man has freeze pops to sell. That sounds wonderful, too. Mark asks his dad to get a freeze pop.

Mark's dad grins and gets him a peach freeze pop. After lunch, Mark gets to play on the playground toys. The best toy at the park is a teeter-totter.

Mark sits on it and asks his dad to sit on the other end. But, Mark's dad is too big. His dad just lifts it up and down. Mark shouts with joy. This is the best fun!

Mark gets off the toy and plops on the ground, glad to have had such fun. Mark hugs his mom and dad and tells them, "This was a wonderful day."

The End

The SoundBlendS Pal

Starling presents

...

The Song Bird

Sounds

wh   ng   ar

oy   oi   igh   ie   ow   ou

ue   oo   ew   ur   ir   er   urr

oa   oe   ee   ea   ai   ay

a e i o u   tch   ch   sh   th

b   bb   c   cc   ck   d   f   ff

g   gg   h   j   k   l   ll   m

mm   n   nn   p   r   s   ss   se

t   tt   v   ve   w   x   z   zz   ze

Words

king   wheels

rung   whispers

sings   wheat

darling   which

eating   whichever

starling   when

wings   whimper

are   a   to   I   of

was   the

In a land far, far away, the first rays of sun are lighting up a town on a big hill. This town is in the kingdom of Jouze. The king of Jouze lives in a high tower at the top of the hill.

The tower has three bronze bells that are ringing a sad song, "Ding, Dong, Ding." And at the top of the tower, the king's blue and silver flag is swaying in the breeze.

In a snug farmhouse just out of town lives a mother with her girls, Ann and Beth. The sun's rays peek into Ann and Beth's room as the sound of the sad bells ring in the girls' ears. "Ding, Dong, Ding."

The bright sunlight and the loud ringing get Ann up. Ann can not remember the bells ringing this way in the past. Ann sees her sister, Beth, in the bed next to hers, still asleep.

Ann gets out **of** her bed and taps her sister on her arm. Beth turns away, tugs **the** covers up past her ears and mutters, "Snooze bar, Ann. I still need **to** sleep."

Ann whispers in Beth's ear, "Beth, get up, now. **The** tower bells **are** ringing." Beth sits up and stretches her arms and legs. Without **the** covers on her ears, **the** bells seem louder.

Then, Beth tells Ann, "This is a problem. The king must not feel well. The bells ring this way when the king is sick." The girls get up. Ann gets on a red dress. Beth gets a blue dress on.

Then, **the** girls run out **to** **the** kitchen. The girls' mom is getting out a pan. Ann goes **to** hug her mom and asks, "Mom, **the** bells **are** ringing. Beth thinks that **the** king is sick. Is that true?"

Her mom frowns, sighs and sets the pan on the counter. Then, Ann and Beth's mom sits on a stool near the kitchen counter and asks the girls to sit down, too.

Then, Ann and Beth's mom tells the girls the news, "When the bells first started ringing, Mistress Olive went up to town to drop off her milk jugs and got the news about the king.

The king is not feeling well. His darling pet goose died last night. The bells are to tell the kingdom that this is a Day of Sadness." Beth cries out, "The Royal Goose died?

That is too bad." Beth starts to sob. Tears drip down her cheeks. Her pet cat, Whiskers, had died just last week. Beth is still sad. Her mom gives her a hug and Ann rubs her back.

Then, Beth tells her mom, "Mom, I have to help the king feel better. When Whiskers died, I felt sad. But, I had lots of help to help ease the pain and loss.

Ann, Mistress Olive, and Nurse Hutch tried **to** help. It **was** wonderful. I still feel sad but I sense that I can help him. If I get him **a** new pet, perhaps **the** king will feel better."

Beth turns to Ann and asks, "Ann, I need help in getting the king a new royal pet. How about a trip to the market?" Ann grins at Beth and tells her, "I think that is a wonderful plan.

Let's eat first, finish **the** clean-up and then set off **to the** market up in town." **The** girls then sit down. Ann and Beth's mom serves them fried eggs and ham with wheat toast.

After eating, the girls rinse off the dishes in the sink. Then, Ann and Beth rush off to brush teeth, and get socks and boots on. Ann braids Beth's long brown hair. Now, the girls are set.

Beth goes into the kitchen and asks her mom, "Mom, may I please have ten silver coins. I need them to get the king a new pet." Beth's mom grins and gets her purse.

After getting **the** silver coins out and handing them **to** Beth, Beth gives her mom **a** tender hug, "This means **a** lot, Mom. I am positive that it will help **the** king **to** feel much, much better."

As Beth is getting the coins, Ann goes out to the barn out back. Ann gets out a harness and a cart to hitch to the goat, Whiz. Ann gets a handful of wheat to feed Whiz as a treat.

Then, Ann wheels **the** cart into his pen. Whiz catches **a** whiff **of** Ann's treat and trots **to** her. Whiz butts Ann's hand. Ann feeds him **a** handful **of** wheat. Whiz seems glad **to** get his treat.

Ann loops **the** harness around him and then attaches him **to the** cart. Just then, Beth skips out **to the** goat pen, singing a joyful song. Beth is glad that Ann is helping her.

Beth helps Ann finish with harnessing Whiz to the cart. The bells stop ringing just as the girls set out. The market is not far. It is held in the town. It is Saturday, and it is Market Day.

The market is held on Market Street each Saturday starting at sun-up. Lots of booths are crowded next to each other. Farmers and merchants sell lots of cool things at the market.

Ann and Beth lead **the** goat cart past **the** farmers' booths. It is hard not **to** stop and get stuff at each booth. **The** stuff is cool. Toys, red ribbons and bright blue dresses **are** on display.

Next to the dress booth, a muffin stand has set up shop. Ann catches a whiff of fresh muffins and asks Beth, "Let's stop and get a snack. The muffins smell terrific. How about it?"

Beth frowns and tells Ann, "I need **to** keep **the** ten silver coins **to** get **the** king's new pet, not muffins." Ann grins at Beth and gets out her purse. In her purse **are** six copper coins.

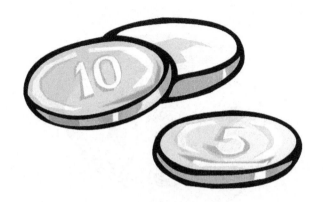

Ann tells her, "Beth, a muffin costs three copper coins. I can get a muffin to split and still keep three copper coins." Beth grins and tells her sister, "That sounds wonderful."

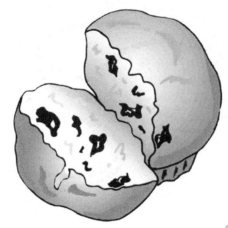

Ann gets a muffin to split with Beth. After eating the snack, the girls lead the goat cart to the pet stands. The merchants are selling lots of different pets.

Beth and Ann see lots **of** fun pets that **the** king might enjoy. Smart dogs that whirl, twirl, and leap on command. Hunting dogs that **are** strong and fast, but still seem sweet.

Black kittens with gray whiskers that whimper and purr as **the** mother cat feeds them. Soft rabbits, which enjoy sitting on laps, sniff at **the** shoppers. Lots and lots **of** wonderful pets.

Beth stops and asks Ann, "Which pet will cheer up **the** king **the** best? Whichever I pick needs **to** help **the** king feel better." Then, next **to the** rabbit stand, Beth catches sight of a songbird.

It is a black starling with green tips on his wings. His song is sweet, high and fast. His singing is joyful and delights the girls. Beth can tell that this is the perfect pet to help cheer up the king.

Beth grabs Ann's arm and points at **the** starling. Ann grins. It is perfect. Beth goes up **to** **the** songbird merchant. **The** merchant is feeding **the** starling bits **of** fresh peach.

With each treat, the starling sings higher and faster. The starling is such a joy to see and hear. Beth asks him, "Pardon us, Sir. But how much is that starling?"

The merchant grins at the girls and tells them, "This is the best songbird that I am selling. It sings lots of fun and wonderful songs. It is thirteen silver coins."

Beth frowns and tells the man, "I need this starling as a gift to the king. It is to cheer him up after his darling pet goose died yesterday. How about ten silver coins?"

The man frowns, thinking about Beth's offer. Ann gets out her three copper coins, too. The girls give **the** coins **to the** merchant. Then, **the** man grins and nods yes.

The man tells the girls, "As the starling is a gift to cheer up the king, it's a deal." The girls cheer. Beth loads up the cart with the starling and the girls set off to see the king.

The king's tower is on top of the hill in the south part of town. As the girls near the king's tower, the bells ring louder. The bells ring long sad sounds that cover the town.

Beth turns **to** Ann and tells her, "Let's speed up. It seems that **the** king is getting sadder." When **the** girls get **to the** king's tower, **a** man stops them.

The man tells the girls, "The king is keeping to himself, today. Visit him on a different day." Beth steps up and tells the man, "Please sir, this is a gift to help the king feel better.

Ann and I wish **to** help out **the** king. It is sad **to** have lost **a** wonderful pet, such as **the** Royal Goose. This is **a** starling with such **a** sweet song that it might bring joy **to** **the** king."

The man peers at the starling and tells the girls, "The king is not allowing visits to his tower today due to the Day of Sadness. But, I wish to hear the songbird sing."

Beth hands a bit of peach to the starling. The starling snatches up the chunk and starts to sing. His singing is high, fast, and sweet. Beth gives him another and the starling sings louder.

Up high in the tower, a sad king hears the starling's sweet, joyful song. At first, it seems just a whisper in the wind. But, as the singing gets louder, the king hears the sweet song.

The sad king leans out his tower and sees the girls with the songbird. The king shouts down to the man, "Let them in." The man sees the king and lets the girls into the tower yard.

The king rushes down to the tower yard and greets the girls. The girls bow at the sight of the king. Beth stands up and tells him, "This songbird is a gift to help on this sad day.

This starling has such a sweet song that it might bring a bit of joy to the royal tower and the king." The king grins and tells the girls, "I am pleased. I will enjoy this gift.

Its song is sweet and lightens this king's sadness." The girls bow and the king gives each of them a royal ring. Beth and Ann gasp at the king's gift. Then, the king hugs each of them.

The girls then lead the goat cart back. Beth and Ann miss the song bird. But each day at noon, the king lets him sing. The girls, the king and the town enjoy his sweet songs.

And, the girls think that helping the king on his Day of Sadness was a wonderful gift in itself.

The End

More Information on **SoundBlends...**

Frequently Asked Questions

How fast should I go through the book?

A good pace is reading one story a week. The stories can be read a little bit each day or all in one sitting.

Sounding out the words seems slow.

Blending Sounds to form Words can seem very slow but this Reading Process is the fastest way to learn to decode! The goal of these stories is to facilitate the Sound-to-Print connection. Be patient. The end result will be wonderful.

Should the reader understand the stories?

A high degree of fluency is needed before the readers will be able to remember the sentences. Fluency is not expected during this program. Reading fluency is a characteristic that needs to be developed after the Sound-to-Print connection has been firmly established. Re-reading the sentences by the teacher (or parent) can be used to help with reading comprehension.

Why are there so few Sight Words?

It is the Sound-to-Print connection that is required to become a fluent reader. Teaching that Words should be memorized by their shape can confuse the reader about the Reading Process → connecting the Letters on the page with the Sounds in the Words.

Frequently Asked Questions

How is SoundBlendS different from Phonics?

In many Phonics programs, not all the Sounds are taught and there can be very little practice in Blending the Sounds to form Words. And there are very few stories that are available that do not make extensive use of Sight Words. SoundBlendS teaches all the Sounds and how to recognize the Letters that represent those Sounds. The Reading Process is obvious and simple for the beginning reader.

Why is reading English so complicated?

English spelling has a long history. It would be easier to teach reading if there was only one symbol (Letter) for each Sound. Several features (using multiple letters for one Sound and using those same letters for more than one Sound) in English spelling do complicate the reading process. SoundBlendS was developed to make these features obvious and simple to the beginning reader.

What should I do if I have questions?

Please look at our website **www.soundblends.com** for more information.

Letter Names

Letters	Letter Names
★ A a	★ Ay
★ B b	★ Bee
★ C c	★ See
★ D d	★ Dee
★ E e	★ Ee
★ F f	★ Eff
★ G g	★ Jee
★ H h	★ Aych
★ I i	★ Igh
★ J j	★ Jay
★ K k	★ Kay
★ L l	★ Ell
★ M m	★ Emm

Letter Names

Letters	Letter Names
★ N n	★ Enn
★ O o	★ Oa
★ P p	★ Pee
★ Q q	★ Kyoo
★ R r	★ Ar
★ S s	★ Ess
★ T t	★ Tee
★ U u	★ Yoo
★ V v	★ Vee
★ W w	★ Dubul-Yoo
★ X x	★ Eks
★ Y y	★ Wigh
★ Z z	★ Zee

Vowel Sounds

	Sound	Spellings
	**a**nt	a
	**e**lephant	e ea ai
	**i**guana	i y ui
	**o**ctopus	o al a
	**u**mbrella	u o o_e ou

Vowel Sounds

	Sound	Spellings
	**jay**	a_e ai a ay ei eigh ey
	**eel**	ea ee y ie ei ey e e_e
	**eye**	i_e ie i y igh eye
	**boat**	o_e o oa ow oe ou ough
	**unicorn**	u_e u ew eu you

Vowel Sounds

	Sound	Spellings
	**h**aw**k**	aw au ough augh
	**m**oo**n**	oo ue ew u ou ui ough
	**b**oo**k**	oul oo u
	**ow**l	ou ow ough
	**oy**ster	oi oy

Vowel Sounds

	Sound	Spellings
	**ar**madillo	ar orr
	b**ir**d	er ur ir or ear ere urr
	**or**ca	or ore oar our oor
	b**ear**	are air arr err ear ere

Consonant Sounds

	Sound	Spellings
	**b**ee	b bb
	**c**at	c k ck ch cc q
	**d**og	d dd ed
	**f**ish	f ff ph gh
	**g**oat	g gg gh gu gue

Consonant Sounds

	Sound	Spellings
	**h**orse	h wh
	**j**aguar	j g ge dge dg
	**l**ion	l ll
	**m**oose	m mm mb mn me
	**n**ewt	n nn gn kn ne

Consonant Sounds

	Sound	Spellings
	**p**anda	p pp
	**r**accoon	r rr wr rh
	**s**eal	s ss sc se c sw
	**t**iger	t tt bt ed th
	**v**iper	v ve

Consonant Sounds

	Sound	Spellings
	**w**olf	w wh
	fo**x**	x
	**y**ak	y
	**z**ebra	z zz ze se s x
	slo**th**	th the

Consonant Sounds

	Sound	Spellings
	**sh**ark	sh sch s
	**ch**icken	ch tch
	ri**ng**	ng
	trea**s**ure	s ss

Combination Sounds

	Sounds	Spellings
	**qu**ail	qu
	cas**tle**	le tle al el ol